GILES DIARY 1994

Ebury Press Stationery

Express Newspapers plc

Personal Details

NAME

Elaine Robinson

ADDRESS

9 Hamilton Road

TELEPHONE (HOME)

TELEPHONE (BUSINESS)

NATIONAL INSURANCE NO.

NATIONAL HEALTH NO.

PASSPORT NO.

DRIVING LICENCE NO.

BANK SORT CODE & ACCOUNT NO.

ADDRESS

TELEPHONE

DOCTOR

ADDRESS

TELEPHONE

DENTIST

TELEPHONE

First published in the United Kingdom in 1993 by
Ebury Press Stationery Limited
Random House, 20 Vauxhall Bridge Road, London SW1V 2SA
Random House UK Limited Reg. No. 954009
Copyright© Random House UK Ltd 1993
Illustrations and captions© Express Newspapers PLC 1993

Whilst every effort has been made to ensure accuracy, the
publishers cannot accept liability for errors.

Calendarial and astronomical data reproduced, with permission,
from data supplied by HM Nautical Almanac Office© copyright
Science and Engineering Research Council.

Set in Gill Roman & Brush Script
by Words and Spaces Limited
Printed in China
Designed by Kim Ludlow
ISBN 0 09 177880 8

Cover Illustration: 1970 Giles Annual (No, 24)

All illustrations and captions taken from original cartoons by Carl Giles

1994 Year Planner

January

M	T	W	T	F	S	S
					1	2
3	4	5	6	7	8	9
10	11	12	13	14	15	16
17	18	19	20	21	22	23
24	25	26	27	28	29	30
31						

February

M	T	W	T	F	S	S
	1	2	3	4	5	6
7	8	9	10	11	12	13
14	15	16	17	18	19	20
21	22	23	24	25	26	27
28						

March

M	T	W	T	F	S	S
	1	2	3	4	5	6
7	8	9	10	11	12	13
14	15	16	17	18	19	20
21	22	23	24	25	26	27
28	29	30	31			

April

M	T	W	T	F	S	S
				1	2	3
4	5	6	7	8	9	10
11	12	13	14	15	16	17
18	19	20	21	22	23	24
25	26	27	28	29	30	

May

M	T	W	T	F	S	S
						1
2	3	4	5	6	7	8
9	10	11	12	13	14	15
16	17	18	19	20	21	22
23	24	25	26	27	28	29
30	31					

June

M	T	W	T	F	S	S
		1	2	3	4	5
6	7	8	9	10	11	12
13	14	15	16	17	18	19
20	21	22	23	24	25	26
27	28	29	30			

July

M	T	W	T	F	S	S
				1	2	3
4	5	6	7	8	9	10
11	12	13	14	15	16	17
18	19	20	21	22	23	24
25	26	27	28	29	30	31

August

M	T	W	T	F	S	S
1	2	3	4	5	6	7
8	9	10	11	12	13	14
15	16	17	18	19	20	21
22	23	24	25	26	27	28
29	30	31				

September

M	T	W	T	F	S	S
			1	2	3	4
5	6	7	8	9	10	11
12	13	14	15	16	17	18
19	20	21	22	23	24	25
26	27	28	29	30		

October

M	T	W	T	F	S	S
					1	2
3	4	5	6	7	8	9
10	11	12	13	14	15	16
17	18	19	20	21	22	23
24	25	26	27	28	29	30
31						

November

M	T	W	T	F	S	S
	1	2	3	4	5	6
7	8	9	10	11	12	13
14	15	16	17	18	19	20
21	22	23	24	25	26	27
28	29	30				

December

M	T	W	T	F	S	S
			1	2	3	4
5	6	7	8	9	10	11
12	13	14	15	16	17	18
19	20	21	22	23	24	25
26	27	28	29	30	31	

1995 Year Planner

January

M	T	W	T	F	S	S
						1
2	3	4	5	6	7	8
9	10	11	12	13	14	15
16	17	18	19	20	21	22
23	24	25	26	27	28	29
30	31					

February

M	T	W	T	F	S	S
		1	2	3	4	5
6	7	8	9	10	11	12
13	14	15	16	17	18	19
20	21	22	23	24	25	26
27	28					

March

M	T	W	T	F	S	S
		1	2	3	4	5
6	7	8	9	10	11	12
13	14	15	16	17	18	19
20	21	22	23	24	25	26
27	28	29	30	31		

April

M	T	W	T	F	S	S
					1	2
3	4	5	6	7	8	9
10	11	12	13	14	15	16
17	18	19	20	21	22	23
24	25	26	27	28	29	30

May

M	T	W	T	F	S	S
1	2	3	4	5	6	7
8	9	10	11	12	13	14
15	16	17	18	19	20	21
22	23	24	25	26	27	28
29	30	31				

June

M	T	W	T	F	S	S
			1	2	3	4
5	6	7	8	9	10	11
12	13	14	15	16	17	18
19	20	21	22	23	24	25
26	27	28	29	30		

July

M	T	W	T	F	S	S
					1	2
3	4	5	6	7	8	9
10	11	12	13	14	15	16
17	18	19	20	21	22	23
24	25	26	27	28	29	30
31						

August

M	T	W	T	F	S	S
1	2	3	4	5	6	
7	8	9	10	11	12	13
14	15	16	17	18	19	20
21	22	23	24	25	26	27
28	29	30	31			

September

M	T	W	T	F	S	S
				1	2	3
4	5	6	7	8	9	10
11	12	13	14	15	16	17
18	19	20	21	22	23	24
25	26	27	28	29	30	

October

M	T	W	T	F	S	S
						1
2	3	4	5	6	7	8
9	10	11	12	13	14	15
16	17	18	19	20	21	22
23	24	25	26	27	28	29
30	31					

November

M	T	W	T	F	S	S
	1	2	3	4	5	
6	7	8	9	10	11	12
13	14	15	16	17	18	19
20	21	22	23	24	25	26
27	28	29	30			

December

M	T	W	T	F	S	S
				1	2	3
4	5	6	7	8	9	10
11	12	13	14	15	16	17
18	19	20	21	22	23	24
25	26	27	28	29	30	31

INTRODUCTION

Carl Giles was born Ronald Giles on 29th September 1916 in London, the son of a tobacconist. Despite leaving school at the age of 13, he soon established himself as a cartoonist at the "Reynolds News" where he attracted the attention of many national newspaper editors but was snapped up by Lord Beaverbrook, then proprietor of Express Newspapers.

The first of his cartoons appeared in the Sunday Express on 3rd October 1943. This hailed the beginning of a relationship that was to span over a period of nearly 40 years.

The first Giles Annual appeared in 1947 and 46 editions have since been published to date and the 47th is under way.

In 1959 Giles was awarded an O.B.E.

December 1993 – January 1994

MONDAY
Holiday
27

TUESDAY
Holiday (exc. USA) ○
28

WEDNESDAY
29

THURSDAY
30

FRIDAY
31

January

M	T	W	T	F	S	S
					1	2
3	4	5	6	7	8	9
10	11	12	13	14	15	16
17	18	19	20	21	22	23
24	25	26	27	28	29	30
31						

SATURDAY
New Year's Day
1

SUNDAY
2

"Your Dad's New Year resolution – jogging. He only got to the end of the road where the police found him in a 'distressed condition' – could you go and pick him up?"

Daily Express, January 2nd, 1986

GILES

January

MONDAY
3

Lowrey Tapestry
Lords & Ladies Tea.

Holiday (subject to confirmation)

TUESDAY
4

Work Shopping £26.04

Holiday Scotland (subject to confirmation)

WEDNESDAY
5

THURSDAY
6 Mavis   Salads £2.00

Epiphany

FRIDAY
7   Meatloaf £2.39

SATURDAY
8   Susan's Visit

SUNDAY
9

January

M	T	W	T	F	S	S
					1	2
3	4	5	6	7	8	9
10	11	12	13	14	15	16
17	18	19	20	21	22	23
24	25	26	27	28	29	30
31						

"Faster, Bert – he's gaining on you."

Sunday Express, December 19th, 1967

MONDAY
10 Row Paul & Debby | over not driving £20
3 Phone calls Debby & Mitchell
(SPEAK NO MORE) home •

TUESDAY
11

WEDNESDAY
12 requested o/d extension £2

THURSDAY
13 £5

FRIDAY
14 Roland rang £3.90

SATURDAY
15 Rachel's 30th Birthday Party. £116 60
Car
allowance

SUNDAY
16

January

M	T	W	T	F	S	S
					1	2
3	4	5	6	7	8	9
10	11	12	13	14	(15)	16
17	18	19	20	21	22	23
24	25	26	27	28	29	30
31						

"By the way – where did we leave the snow plough last year?"

Daily Express, November 16th, 1982

GILES

January

MONDAY
17
Holiday USA (Martin Luther King's Birthday)

TUESDAY
18

WEDNESDAY
19

THURSDAY
20

FRIDAY
21

SATURDAY
22

SUNDAY
23

January

M	T	W	T	F	S	S
					1	2
3	4	5	6	7	8	9
10	11	12	13	14	15	16
17	18	19	20	21	22	23
24	25	26	27	28	29	30
31						

"Never mind about the neighbours thinking you're soliciting if you
have a light in the porch – switch the bloody thing on!"

Sunday Express, February 8th, 1976

January

MONDAY
24

TUESDAY
25

WEDNESDAY
26   Auntie   Pay Day
Evelyn

Australia Day

THURSDAY
27

FRIDAY
28

January

M	T	W	T	F	S	S
					1	2
3	4	5	6	7	8	9
10	11	12	13	14	15	16
17	18	19	20	21	22	23
24	25	26	27	28	29	30
31						

SATURDAY
29

SUNDAY
30

"Good morning, Porky...O symbol of Peace and Tranquillity."

Daily Express, February 15th, 1983

January – February

MONDAY
31

TUESDAY
1

WEDNESDAY
2 M

THURSDAY
3

FRIDAY
4 Mother

SATURDAY
5

February

M	T	W	T	F	S	S
	1	2	3	4	5	6
7	8	9	10	11	12	13
14	15	16	17	18	19	20
21	22	23	24	25	26	27
28						

SUNDAY   Waitangi Day, NZ   Accession of Queen Elizabeth II
6

"Bravo! You've beaten Eddie Edwards' record 58th place out of 58 – you're 59th."

Daily Express, February 18th, 1988

GILES

MONDAY

7

TUESDAY

8

WEDNESDAY

9

THURSDAY

10 ●

FRIDAY

11

SATURDAY Ramadan begins (subject to sighting of the moon)   Holiday USA (Lincoln's Birthday)

12

SUNDAY

13

February

M	T	W	T	F	S	S
	1	2	3	4	5	6
7	8	9	10	11	12	13
14	15	16	17	18	19	20
21	22	23	24	25	26	27
28						

"Ask your mother to stop telling me this three-mile walk to Auntie Vi's will do me good."

Sunday Express, February 5th, 1978

February

MONDAY
14 *Eon*   St Valentine's Day

TUESDAY
15   Shrove Tuesday

WEDNESDAY
16   Ash Wednesday

THURSDAY
17

FRIDAY
18   ◗

SATURDAY
19

February

M	T	W	T	F	S	S
	1	2	3	4	5	6
7	8	9	10	11	12	13
14	15	16	17	18	19	20
21	22	23	24	25	26	27
28						

SUNDAY
20

"If they keep on bombing Germany, their railways will soon be as bad as ours, won't they, sir?"

Sunday Express, February 4th, 1945

February

MONDAY
21
Holiday USA (President's Day)

TUESDAY
22
George Washington's Birthday

WEDNESDAY
23

THURSDAY
24

FRIDAY
25

SATURDAY
26
○

SUNDAY
27

February

M	T	W	T	F	S	S
	1	2	3	4	5	6
7	8	9	10	11	12	13
14	15	16	17	18	19	20
21	22	23	24	25	26	27
28						

"Okay – switch on."

Daily Express, February 15th, 1978

GILES

MONDAY
28

TUESDAY   St David's Day
1

WEDNESDAY
2

THURSDAY
3

FRIDAY   ◑
4

SATURDAY
5

March

M	T	W	T	F	S	S
	1	2	3	4	5	6
7	8	9	10	11	12	13
14	15	16	17	18	19	20
21	22	23	24	25	26	27
28	29	30	31			

SUNDAY
6

"Welcome back, Dawn Chorus – the oppressive silence was killing me!"

Daily Express, March 1st, 1984

GILES

March

MONDAY
7

TUESDAY
8

WEDNESDAY
9

THURSDAY
10

FRIDAY
11

SATURDAY
12
Islamic Festival of Eid-ul-Fitre (subject to sighting of the moon) ●

SUNDAY
13
Mothers' Day UK

March

M	T	W	T	F	S	S
	1	2	3	4	5	6
7	8	9	10	11	12	13
14	15	16	17	18	19	20
21	22	23	24	25	26	27
28	29	30	31			

"Take these in to your dad to give me for Mother's Day."

Sunday Express, March 10th, 1991

March

MONDAY
14
Commonwealth Day

TUESDAY
15

WEDNESDAY
16

THURSDAY
17
St Patrick's Day Holiday N. Ireland

FRIDAY
18

SATURDAY
19

SUNDAY
20
Vernal Equinox ◗

March

M	T	W	T	F	S	S
	1	2	3	4	5	6
7	8	9	10	11	12	13
14	15	16	17	18	19	20
21	22	23	24	25	26	27
28	29	30	31			

"Well, Madam, if you have definitely decided not to vote for me what am I doing nursing your baby?

Sunday Express, February 12th, 1950

March

MONDAY
21

TUESDAY
22

WEDNESDAY
23

THURSDAY
24

FRIDAY
25

SATURDAY
26

March

M	T	W	T	F	S	S
	1	2	3	4	5	6
7	8	9	10	11	12	13
14	15	16	17	18	19	20
21	22	23	24	25	26	27
28	29	30	31			

SUNDAY   Palm Sunday   Jewish Festival of Passover (Pesach) First Day   British Summertime begins   ○
27

"I don't think there'll be much trouble kidnapping him – it's whether you'll get anything for him."

Daily Express, March 26th, 1981

GILES

MONDAY
28

TUESDAY
29

WEDNESDAY
30

THURSDAY
31   Maundy Thursday

FRIDAY
1   Good Friday Holiday

SATURDAY
2   Jewish Festival of Passover (Pesach) Seventh Day

SUNDAY
3   Easter Day   Daylight Saving Time begins, USA ◗

April

M	T	W	T	F	S	S
				1	2	3
4	5	6	7	8	9	10
11	12	13	14	15	16	17
18	19	20	21	22	23	24
25	26	27	28	29	30	

"You could just say 'Happy Easter' to them."

Sunday Express, March 31st, 1991

April

MONDAY

Easter Monday Holiday (exc. Scotland)

4

TUESDAY

5

WEDNESDAY

6

THURSDAY

7

FRIDAY

8

SATURDAY

9

SUNDAY

10

April

M	T	W	T	F	S	S
				1	2	3
4	5	6	7	8	9	10
11	12	13	14	15	16	17
18	19	20	21	22	23	24
25	26	27	28	29	30	

"Damn flowers – never a bottle of Scotch."

Sunday Express, March 21st, 1971

GILES

MONDAY
11

TUESDAY
12

WEDNESDAY
13

THURSDAY
14

FRIDAY
15

SATURDAY
16

SUNDAY
17

April

M	T	W	T	F	S	S
				1	2	3
4	5	6	7	8	9	10
11	12	13	14	15	16	17
18	19	20	21	22	23	24
25	26	27	28	29	30	

"When I said it's time we got the garden things out for Spring I was thinking more in the line of these."

Sunday Express, March 20th, 1988

GALES

MONDAY
18

TUESDAY ◗
19

WEDNESDAY
20

THURSDAY   Queen Elizabeth II's Birthday
21

FRIDAY
22

SATURDAY   St George's Day
23

SUNDAY
24

April

M	T	W	T	F	S	S
				1	2	3
4	5	6	7	8	9	10
11	12	13	14	15	16	17
18	19	20	21	22	23	24
25	26	27	28	29	30	

"Good morning, Madam, aren't we the lady that got done for sending
Her Majesty six British Railway spoons for her Silver Wedding?"

Daily Express, April 20th, 1976

April – May

MONDAY
25
Holiday Australia, NZ (Anzac Day) ○

TUESDAY
26

WEDNESDAY
27

THURSDAY
28

FRIDAY
29

May

M	T	W	T	F	S	S
						1
2	3	4	5	6	7	8
9	10	11	12	13	14	15
16	17	18	19	20	21	22
23	24	25	26	27	28	29
30	31					

SATURDAY
30

SUNDAY
1

"I told you not to trust her with the mower after her horse refused at the first fence."

Sunday Express, April 7th, 1991

GALES

May

MONDAY

May Day Holiday UK (exc. Scotland)   Spring Holiday Scotland   ◑

2

TUESDAY

3

WEDNESDAY

4

THURSDAY

5

FRIDAY

6

May

M	T	W	T	F	S	S
						1
2	3	4	5	6	7	8
9	10	11	12	13	14	15
16	17	18	19	20	21	22
23	24	25	26	27	28	29
30	31					

SATURDAY

7

SUNDAY

Mothers' Day USA

8

"There goes the Mother's Day cake we baked for Grandma."

Sunday Express, April 1st, 1984

May

MONDAY
9

TUESDAY
10 ●

WEDNESDAY
11

THURSDAY
12   Ascension Day

FRIDAY
13

SATURDAY
14

SUNDAY
15

May

M	T	W	T	F	S	S
						1
2	3	4	5	6	7	8
9	10	11	12	13	14	15
16	17	18	19	20	21	22
23	24	25	26	27	28	29
30	31					

"All these long sunny walks dad's taking us on – we'll get ever so brown."

May

MONDAY
Jewish Feast of Weeks (Shavuot)
16

TUESDAY
17

WEDNESDAY   ◐
18

THURSDAY
19

FRIDAY
20

May

M	T	W	T	F	S	S
						1
2	3	4	5	6	7	8
9	10	11	12	13	14	15
16	17	18	19	20	21	22
23	24	25	26	27	28	29
30	31					

SATURDAY
21

SUNDAY
Whit Sunday
22

"Just until he makes his mind up."

Daily Express, April 30th, 1981

GILES

May

MONDAY
23
Holiday Canada (Victoria Day)

TUESDAY
24

WEDNESDAY
25
○

THURSDAY
26

FRIDAY
27

May

M	T	W	T	F	S	S
						1
2	3	4	5	6	7	8
9	10	11	12	13	14	15
16	17	18	19	20	21	22
23	24	25	26	27	28	29
30	31					

SATURDAY
28

SUNDAY
29
Trinity Sunday

"Unconfirmed report that one of your jump-jets has made a direct hit on Dad's cornflakes."

Daily Express, May 4th, 1982

May – June

MONDAY
30

Spring Holiday UK (exc. Scotland)   May Day Holiday Scotland   Holiday USA (Memorial Day)

TUESDAY
31

WEDNESDAY
1

THURSDAY
2

Corpus Christi   Coronation Day

FRIDAY
3

SATURDAY
4

SUNDAY
5

June

M	T	W	T	F	S	S
		1	2	3	4	5
6	7	8	9	10	11	12
13	14	15	16	17	18	19
20	21	22	23	24	25	26
27	28	29	30			

"Hurry up, Mr Marathon – the other 20,141 left twenty minutes ago."

Sunday Express, May 13th, 1984

GALES

June

MONDAY
Holiday NZ (Queen Elizabeth II's Birthday)

6

TUESDAY

7

WEDNESDAY

8

THURSDAY
●

9

FRIDAY
Islamic New Year begins (subject to sighting of the moon)

10

SATURDAY

11

SUNDAY

12

June

M	T	W	T	F	S	S
		1	2	3	4	5
6	7	8	9	10	11	12
13	14	15	16	17	18	19
20	21	22	23	24	25	26
27	28	29	30			

"Know what he'll give me? He'll give me: 'Lord Brabazon told the Minister of Transport that it should be an offence for one person to occupy a car by himself.'"

Daily Express, May 24th, 1960

GILES

June

MONDAY
13

TUESDAY
14

WEDNESDAY
15

THURSDAY
16

FRIDAY
17

SATURDAY
18

SUNDAY
19

Fathers' Day UK, USA

June

M	T	W	T	F	S	S
			1	2	3	4	5
6	7	8	9	10	11	12
13	14	15	16	17	18	19
20	21	22	23	24	25	26
27	28	29	30			

"Awake my love, 'tis Father's Day – for a special treat you've got football all the afternoon on TV."

Sunday Express, June 20th, 1982

June

MONDAY

20

TUESDAY

21

Summer Solstice

WEDNESDAY

22

THURSDAY

23

○

FRIDAY

24

SATURDAY

25

SUNDAY

26

June

M	T	W	T	F	S	S
		1	2	3	4	5
6	7	8	9	10	11	12
13	14	15	16	17	18	19
20	21	22	23	24	25	26
27	28	29	30			

Flaming June.

Daily Express, June 21st, 1960

MONDAY
27

TUESDAY
28

WEDNESDAY
29

THURSDAY   ◑
30

FRIDAY   Holiday Canada (Canada Day)
1

SATURDAY
2

SUNDAY
3

July

M	T	W	T	F	S	S
				1	2	3
4	5	6	7	8	9	10
11	12	13	14	15	16	17
18	19	20	21	22	23	24
25	26	27	28	29	30	31

"Smile, please."

Sunday Express, June 29th, 1958

GILES

July

MONDAY
4
Holiday USA (Independence Day)

TUESDAY
5

WEDNESDAY
6

THURSDAY
7

FRIDAY
8
●

SATURDAY
9

SUNDAY
10

July

M	T	W	T	F	S	S
				1	2	3
4	5	6	7	8	9	10
11	12	13	14	15	16	17
18	19	20	21	22	23	24
25	26	27	28	29	30	31

"I'm not taking you to court over who owns it, but it'll be the Old Bailey for the pair of you
if I catch it near my goldfish pond again."

Sunday Express, June 17th, 1984

July

MONDAY
11

TUESDAY   Battle of the Boyne Holiday N. Ireland
12

WEDNESDAY
13

THURSDAY
14

FRIDAY   St Swithin's Day
15

SATURDAY   ◖
16

SUNDAY
17

July

M	T	W	T	F	S	S
				1	2	3
4	5	6	7	8	9	10
11	12	13	14	15	16	17
18	19	20	21	22	23	24
25	26	27	28	29	30	31

"Here we go again – every time BP sticks the price up, it's: Carol! Have you seen the pony?"

Daily Express, June 11th, 1981

July

MONDAY
18

TUESDAY
19

WEDNESDAY
20

THURSDAY
21

FRIDAY
22   ○

SATURDAY
23

SUNDAY
24

July

M	T	W	T	F	S	S
				1	2	3
4	5	6	7	8	9	10
11	12	13	14	15	16	17
18	19	20	21	22	23	24
25	26	27	28	29	30	31

"And this comment from your music teacher – 'I hope your boy enjoys his holiday as much as I'm going to enjoy mine'..."

Sunday Express, July 21st, 1968

July

MONDAY
25

TUESDAY
26

WEDNESDAY
27

THURSDAY
28

FRIDAY
29

SATURDAY
30

SUNDAY
31

July

M	T	W	T	F	S	S
				1	2	3
4	5	6	7	8	9	10
11	12	13	14	15	16	17
18	19	20	21	22	23	24
25	26	27	28	29	30	31

"I hope this silly game isn't a stunt to divert my attentions from one of your tricks."

Sunday Express, July 11th, 1965

August

MONDAY
1
Summer Bank Holiday Scotland

TUESDAY
2

WEDNESDAY
3

THURSDAY
4

FRIDAY
5

SATURDAY
6

August

M	T	W	T	F	S	S
1	2	3	4	5	6	7
8	9	10	11	12	13	14
15	16	17	18	19	20	21
22	23	24	25	26	27	28
29	30	31				

SUNDAY
7

●

"If your licence does go up to £10, in future the slippers will be delivered right here."

Sunday Express, July 8th, 1984

GILES

August

MONDAY

8

TUESDAY

9

WEDNESDAY

10

THURSDAY

11

FRIDAY

12

SATURDAY

13

SUNDAY

14

August

M	T	W	T	F	S	S
1	2	3	4	5	6	7
8	9	10	11	12	13	14
15	16	17	18	19	20	21
22	23	24	25	26	27	28
29	30	31				

"Dad, remember the gentleman you hit for playing his saxophone all the time
we were delayed at Gatwick?"

Sunday Express, August 30th, 1987

August

MONDAY
15

TUESDAY
16

WEDNESDAY
17

THURSDAY
18

FRIDAY
19

SATURDAY
20

SUNDAY
21

August

M	T	W	T	F	S	S
1	2	3	4	5	6	7
8	9	10	11	12	13	14
15	16	17	18	19	20	21
22	23	24	25	26	27	28
29	30	31				

"We know all about Madonna throwing hers into the crowd – put your back on at once."

Daily Express, August 13th, 1987

August

MONDAY
22

TUESDAY
23

WEDNESDAY
24

THURSDAY
25

FRIDAY
26

SATURDAY
27

SUNDAY
28

August

M	T	W	T	F	S	S
1	2	3	4	5	6	7
8	9	10	11	12	13	14
15	16	17	18	19	20	21
22	23	24	25	26	27	28
29	30	31				

"It's a summons from a burglar who broke in and stole half a bottle of Grandma's home-made wine and has never been the same since."

Sunday Express, September 26th, 1982

GILES

August – September

MONDAY
29
Summer Bank Holiday (exc. Scotland) ◑

TUESDAY
30

WEDNESDAY
31

THURSDAY
1

FRIDAY
2

SATURDAY
3

September

M	T	W	T	F	S	S
			1	2	3	4
5	6	7	8	9	10	11
12	13	14	15	16	17	18
19	20	21	22	23	24	25
26	27	28	29	30		

SUNDAY
4

"Give me the old exotic baked beans and bangers any day."

Daily Express, September 13th, 1966

GALES

September

MONDAY
5
Holiday USA (Labor Day)   Holiday Canada (Labour Day)   ●

TUESDAY
6

WEDNESDAY
7

THURSDAY
8

FRIDAY
9

SATURDAY
10

September

M	T	W	T	F	S	S
			1	2	3	4
5	6	7	8	9	10	11
12	13	14	15	16	17	18
19	20	21	22	23	24	25
26	27	28	29	30		

SUNDAY
11

"Anything that gets in as late as him I'd flog to British Rail."

Sunday Express, October 17th, 1982

September

MONDAY
12

TUESDAY
13

WEDNESDAY
14

THURSDAY
15

Jewish Day of Atonement (Yom Kippur)

FRIDAY
16

SATURDAY
17

SUNDAY
18

September

M	T	W	T	F	S	S
			1	2	3	4
5	6	7	8	9	10	11
12	13	14	15	16	17	18
19	20	21	22	23	24	25
26	27	28	29	30		

"Do you think you could manage to lift his Teddy off the floor for him?"

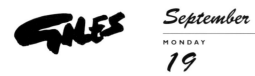

September

MONDAY
19

○

TUESDAY
20
Jewish Festival of Tabernacles (Succoth) First Day

WEDNESDAY
21

THURSDAY
22

FRIDAY
23
Autumnal Equinox

SATURDAY
24

SUNDAY
25

September

M	T	W	T	F	S	S
			1	2	3	4
5	6	7	8	9	10	11
12	13	14	15	16	17	18
19	20	21	22	23	24	25
26	27	28	29	30		

"Latest order from Brussels – carrots are now called 'fruit'."

Sunday Express, November 11th, 1990

GILES

September – October

MONDAY
26

TUESDAY
27

WEDNESDAY
28

THURSDAY
29

FRIDAY
30

SATURDAY
1

SUNDAY
2

October

M	T	W	T	F	S	S
					1	2
3	4	5	6	7	8	9
10	11	12	13	14	15	16
17	18	19	20	21	22	23
24	25	26	27	28	29	30
31						

"Madam would go a long way towards improving her public relationship with the police
if she would kindly remove her car from my foot."

Daily Express, November 20th, 1959

GALES

October

MONDAY
3

TUESDAY
4

WEDNESDAY
5   ●

THURSDAY
6

FRIDAY
7

SATURDAY
8

SUNDAY
9

October

M	T	W	T	F	S	S
					1	2
3	4	5	6	7	8	9
10	11	12	13	14	15	16
17	18	19	20	21	22	23
24	25	26	27	28	29	30
31						

"Dad, you know the Consumers Association said a goose is a better guard dog than a dog?"

Daily Express, November 24th, 1981

October

MONDAY
10

Holiday USA (Columbus Day)   Holiday Canada (Thanksgiving)

TUESDAY
11

WEDNESDAY
12

THURSDAY
13

FRIDAY
14

SATURDAY
15

SUNDAY
16

October

M	T	W	T	F	S	S
					1	2
3	4	5	6	7	8	9
10	11	12	13	14	15	16
17	18	19	20	21	22	23
24	25	26	27	28	29	30
31						

"If Grandma's bought a short dress I'm going to leave home."

Daily Express, January 31st, 1958

GILES

October

MONDAY
17

TUESDAY
18

WEDNESDAY
19

○

THURSDAY
20

FRIDAY
21

October

M	T	W	T	F	S	S
					1	2
3	4	5	6	7	8	9
10	11	12	13	14	15	16
17	18	19	20	21	22	23
24	25	26	27	28	29	30
31						

SATURDAY
22

SUNDAY
23

British Summertime ends

"Right. You've convinced me you can walk a straight line for a mile –
now come back to the station while I charge you."

Daily Express, December 21st, 1962

October

MONDAY
24
Holiday NZ (Labour Day)

TUESDAY
25

WEDNESDAY
26

THURSDAY
27
◑

FRIDAY
28

October

M	T	W	T	F	S	S
					1	2
3	4	5	6	7	8	9
10	11	12	13	14	15	16
17	18	19	20	21	22	23
24	25	26	27	28	29	30
31						

SATURDAY
29

SUNDAY
30
Daylight Saving Time ends, USA

"She's not kerb-crawling in your sense of the word, Sir, she uses the kerb to find her way home."

Sunday Express, January 27th, 1985

October – November

MONDAY Hallowe'en
31

TUESDAY All Saints' Day
1

WEDNESDAY
2

THURSDAY ●
3

FRIDAY
4

SATURDAY Guy Fawkes' Day
5

SUNDAY
6

November

M	T	W	T	F	S	S
		1	2	3	4	5	6
7	8	9	10	11	12	13
14	15	16	17	18	19	20
21	22	23	24	25	26	27
28	29	30				

"I shouldn't put that one in, Sir – that's Mr. Wilmot, the maths master."

Daily Express, October 28th, 1977

GILES

November

MONDAY
7

TUESDAY
8

WEDNESDAY
9

THURSDAY ☽
10

Holiday USA (Veterans' Day)   Holiday Canada (Remembrance Day)

FRIDAY
11

SATURDAY
12

November

M	T	W	T	F	S	S
	1	2	3	4	5	6
7	8	9	10	11	12	13
14	15	16	17	18	19	20
21	22	23	24	25	26	27
28	29	30				

Remembrance Sunday

SUNDAY
13

"To avoid some grievous bodily harm get Grandma out by the back door before she sees who's just come in."

Sunday Express, September 25th, 1988

MONDAY

14

TUESDAY

15

WEDNESDAY

16

THURSDAY

17

FRIDAY

18

○

SATURDAY

19

SUNDAY

20

November

M	T	W	T	F	S	S
	1	2	3	4	5	6
7	8	9	10	11	12	13
14	15	16	17	18	19	20
21	22	23	24	25	26	27
28	29	30				

"The rest of the boys decided to open up a delivery service."

Daily Express, February 2nd, 1976

November

MONDAY
21

TUESDAY
22

WEDNESDAY
23

THURSDAY
24
Holiday USA (Thanksgiving)

FRIDAY
25

SATURDAY
26

SUNDAY
27
First Sunday in Advent

November

M	T	W	T	F	S	S
	1	2	3	4	5	6
7	8	9	10	11	12	13
14	15	16	17	18	19	20
21	22	23	24	25	26	27
28	29	30				

"You've bought Grandma a WHAT for Christmas?"

Sunday Express, December 21st, 1980

MONDAY

28

Jewish Festival of Chanukah (First Day)

TUESDAY

29

WEDNESDAY

30

St Andrew's Day

THURSDAY

1

FRIDAY

2

●

SATURDAY

3

December

M	T	W	T	F	S	S
			1	2	3	4
5	6	7	8	9	10	11
12	13	14	15	16	17	18
19	20	21	22	23	24	25
26	27	28	29	30	31	

SUNDAY

4

"I told you a small open boat was false economy. We should have had the one with the cabin."

Daily Express, January 11th, 1968

Gales

December

MONDAY
5

TUESDAY
6

WEDNESDAY
7

THURSDAY
8

FRIDAY ◗
9

SATURDAY
10

SUNDAY
11

December

M	T	W	T	F	S	S
			1	2	3	4
5	6	7	8	9	10	11
12	13	14	15	16	17	18
19	20	21	22	23	24	25
26	27	28	29	30	31	

"Mum! Grandma's gone down behind the piano."

Daily Express, December 28th, 1974

GILES

December

MONDAY
12

TUESDAY
13

WEDNESDAY
14

THURSDAY
15

FRIDAY
16

SATURDAY
17

SUNDAY
18

December

M	T	W	T	F	S	S
			1	2	3	4
5	6	7	8	9	10	11
12	13	14	15	16	17	18
19	20	21	22	23	24	25
26	27	28	29	30	31	

"Never mind who hit who first – put the boy down."

Daily Express, December 14th, 1965

December

MONDAY
19

TUESDAY
20

WEDNESDAY
21

THURSDAY
22   Winter Solstice

FRIDAY
23

December

M	T	W	T	F	S	S
			1	2	3	4
5	6	7	8	9	10	11
12	13	14	15	16	17	18
19	20	21	22	23	24	25
26	27	28	29	30	31	

SATURDAY
24   Christmas Eve

SUNDAY
25   Christmas Day ◑

"Hold it, Dad — Auntie Ivy hasn't quite gone yet."

Daily Express, December 28th, 1967

MONDAY

26

Boxing Day Holiday

TUESDAY

27

Holiday (subject to confirmation)

WEDNESDAY

28

THURSDAY

29

FRIDAY

30

January 1995

M	T	W	T	F	S	S
						1
2	3	4	5	6	7	8
9	10	11	12	13	14	15
16	17	18	19	20	21	22
23	24	25	26	27	28	29
30	31					

SATURDAY

31

SUNDAY

1

New Year's Day

"'George,' I said, 'Christmas Eve. What better time to ask our new neighbours round for a drink and meet Mummy'."

Daily Express, December 24, 1974

January 1995

MONDAY   Holiday

2

TUESDAY   Holiday, Scotland

3

WEDNESDAY

4

THURSDAY

5

FRIDAY   Epiphany

6

January 1995

M	T	W	T	F	S	S
						1
2	3	4	5	6	7	8
9	10	11	12	13	14	15
16	17	18	19	20	21	22
23	24	25	26	27	28	29
30	31					

SATURDAY

7

SUNDAY

8